The Welsh Language

Cennard Davies

y Lolfa

First impression: 2006
© Cennard Davies and Y Lolfa Cyf., 2006

We are grateful to the following for permission to reproduce
photographs: Nant Gwrtheyrn National Language Centre,
The National Library of Wales, Gerallt Llywelyn,
Menter Iaith Rhondda Cynon Taf, Public Records Office,
Adrian Parsons, S4C, Tegwyn Roberts

Cover design: Y Lolfa

SBN: 0 86243 866 7

Printed on acid-free and partly recycled paper
and published and bound in Wales by
Y Lolfa Cyf., Talybont, Ceredigion SY24 5AP
e-mail ylolfa@ylolfa.com
website www.ylolfa.com
tel (01970) 832 304
fax 832 782

Contents

Contents

The Family of Languages

How is Welsh related to other languages?

By now, we accept that languages are related to one another. We say that Welsh is a Celtic language and that it belongs to the same group of languages as Breton and Irish. Similarly, we call Spanish and French Romance languages, which have developed from Latin. Indeed, we sometimes speak of families of languages. But, did you know that it was a man whose family came from Anglesey who first suggested that most European and many Asian languages were interrelated? To explain this, he claimed that they had all developed initially from an ancient language that we now call Indo-European.

The name of this remarkable man was William Jones. Oddly enough, his father also bore the same name. They lived in the 18th century, and both father and son achieved eminence, but in very different fields of study. William Jones, senior, was an able mathematician, a friend of the famous scientist, Sir Isaac Newton, and a Fellow of the Royal Society. Although he was born in Llanfihangel Tre'r Beirdd on Anglesey, he spent most of his life in England. It was there that his son was born.

Although the younger William Jones studied law and became a judge in Bengal, India, languages were his main field of interest. He had learned Greek and Latin before going to India, but, while he was there, he had an opportunity to study the oldest language of the Indian sub-continent, Sanskrit.

William Jones noticed that there were striking similarities between the three languages, although they belonged to different continents. How could this be explained? He decided that many of the languages of Europe and Asia had developed from a common ancestral language, and he outlined his theory for the first time at a meeting of the Bengal Asian Society in 1786.

Towards the end of the eighteenth century, philologists began to study groups of languages. They showed, for example, that French, Spanish and Italian had developed from Latin. They were able to prove that *padre* (Italian), *padre* (Spanish), *père* (French), *pai* (Portuguese) and *pare* (Catalan) had all developed from the Latin word for father, *pater*.

According to Sir William Jones, the same process had occurred when Indo-European developed into different languages throughout Europe and Asia. Of course, not one word of Indo-European has survived, but linguists believe that the people who spoke the language lived about 6000 years ago. From their original home in southern Russia they migrated eastward and westward, reaching central Europe by 3500 BC and India by 2000 BC.

From this original language, there developed nine families of languages. One of these was Celtic, and it is to this group, as we shall see, that Welsh belongs. In speaking of Sir William Jones, we should note one interesting tale about him. Once, while on a visit to Paris, he was introduced to the French King by the British Ambassador. In presenting him, the ambassador said, "Sir William is a very strange man. He can speak practically every language under the sun, except his own!"

This was perfectly true, for although he could read a little Welsh, he was unable to speak the language!

THE INDO-EUROPEAN FAMILY TREE

Indo-European

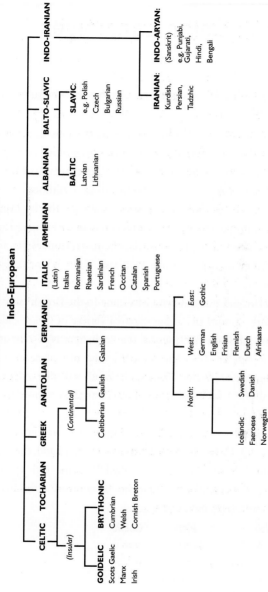

CELTIC **TOCHARIAN** **GREEK** **ANATOLIAN** **GERMANIC** **ITALIC** **ARMENIAN** **ALBANIAN** **BALTO-SLAVIC** **INDO-IRANIAN**

(Insular) *(Continental)*

GOIDELIC
Scots Gaelic
Manx
Irish

BRYTHONIC
Cumbrian
Welsh
Cornish Breton

Celtiberian Gaulish
Galatian

GERMANIC

North:
Icelandic
Faeroese
Norwegian
Swedish
Danish

West:
German
English
Frisian
Flemish
Dutch
Afrikaans

East:
Gothic

ITALIC
(Latin)
Italian
Romanian
Rhaetian
Sardinian
French
Occitan
Catalan
Spanish
Portuguese

BALTIC
Latvian
Lithuanian

SLAVIC:
e.g. Polish
Czech
Bulgarian
Russian

INDO-ARYAN:
(Sanskrit)
e.g. Punjabi,
Gujarati,
Hindi,
Bengali

IRANIAN:
Kurdish,
Persian,
Tadzhic

The Celtic Languages

How many Celtic languages are there and how are they related?

Around the 5th century BC, people whom the Greeks referred to as 'Keltoi' lived in central Europe. From there, they dispersed throughout the Continent, as far as the Black Sea and Asia Minor, south-west Spain, central Italy and the British Isles. Although there are now no people, apart from the Bretons, speaking Celtic languages on mainland Europe, many place names and names of rivers prove that Celts once lived there. Rivers such as Donau (Danube), Rhone and Rhine (Rhein) and cities like Paris and Wien (Vienna) are a case in point.

It was to Ireland that the first Celts came to the British Isles, in about the fifth century BC. They spoke a variety of Celtic called Goidelic, and it is from that language that Irish, Scottish Gaelic and Manx developed. At a later date, a further wave of settlers came to southern England and Wales. These spoke another branch of Celtic, namely Brythonic, and Welsh, Breton and Cornish developed from this language.

As Goidelic had retained the Indo-European 'kw' sound, it is referred to as 'Q' Celtic. In Brythonic, on the other hand, the 'kw' sound became 'p' and, as a result, it is called 'P' Celtic. One can see the difference between the two branches by comparing this list of words in Welsh, Irish and Scots Gaelic:

Welsh	Irish	Gaelic
pen (*head*)	ceann	ceann
pwy? (*who?*)	cé?	cò?
pedwar (*four*)	ceathair	ceithir

Apart from Welsh, the other Celtic languages are:

Cornish

Although some enthusiasts are now trying to revive Cornish, it ceased to be a living language in the eighteenth century. According to some people, Dorothy Pentreath, who died in 1777, was the last person to speak Cornish as a mother tongue.

Breton

As the French government Census doesn't require citizens to record whether or not they are able to speak Breton, we don't know how many are able to speak the language today. It was quite strong in the 1940s, with about a million speakers. By now, however, it is possible that the number of speakers is less than half that figure. Although Breton doesn't have official status, some schools teach through the medium of the language, and *Diwan*, a movement similar to *Mudiad Ysgolion Meithrin* (The Welsh Playgroup Movement), is growing.

Irish

Almost everybody in Ireland spoke Irish up to the seventeenth century, but the growth of English influence and the 1845-49 famine did great damage to the language. By the time that Ireland won its independence in 1922, the country was almost completely anglicised. By today, only about 30,000 people use Irish as their habitual means of communication, mainly in the Gaeltacht, or Irish-speaking areas of Connemara and Donegal. However, many more are able to speak the language, as it has been taught in schools since 1922. There is increasing interest in Irish and its literature at the present time, and the number of schools teaching through the medium of the language has grown. *Raidio na Gaeltachta,* the Irish language radio station, broadcasts throughout the country, and there is also an Irish language television channel.

Scottish Gaelic

According to the 2001 Census, 58,650 people speak Scottish Gaelic, most of whom live in the Western Isles. Since the 1991 Census, the language has seen a decline of 11%. By now, very little Gaelic is spoken on the mainland, but interest in the language is growing. The number of Gaelic-medium schools is increasing and there are more programmes on radio and television. There are also a number of interesting writers emerging.

Manx

A Welshman, Bishop John Phillips, was the first to write anything in the Manx language, when he translated the Book of Common Prayer in 1610. There was a rapid decrease in the number of speakers during the 19th century and, by the 1901 Census, only 4,419 were able to speak the language. It soon ceased to function as a living language, but as in the case of Cornish, there are some enthusiasts seeking to revive it.

Welsh Throughout the Ages

How has Welsh changed over the centuries?

We usually divide the history of the Welsh language into four main periods:

i) Early Welsh (–850)
ii) Old Welsh (850–1100)
iii) Middle Welsh (1100–1400)
iv) Modern Welsh (1400–)

EARLY WELSH

Sometime between the middle of the fifth century and the end of the sixth, the Brythonic language had developed into Welsh. While Brythonic, like Latin, changed word endings to convey meaning, Welsh used the position of words, or prepositions, for this purpose. During this process of change, Brythonic words lost their endings, thus:

> ★ marcos > march (a stallion)
> ★ bardos > bardd (a poet)
> ★ nemos > nef (heaven)
> ★ mapos > mab (son)

When this occurred, the period known as Early Welsh began, and it lasted from the birth of the new language to 850.

Naturally, very little Welsh from this period has survived – only a seventh century inscription on a memorial stone in Tywyn Church, a few place names and personal names in the works of the Venerable

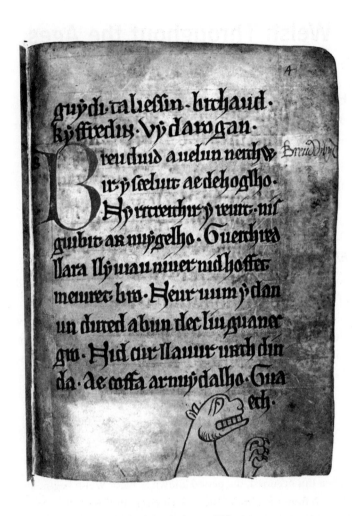

A page from the Black Book of Carmarthen, a 13th century manuscript

Bede, together with a little Early Welsh in the Book of St. Chad, a copy of the gospels in Latin compiled about the end of the seventh century. This book contains a copy of a sixth century Welsh deed, recording a dispute over land. This is the oldest extant document written in Welsh.

OLD WELSH

More examples of Old Welsh have survived. Many of these are in the form of marginal notes explaining the meaning of Latin words, but in the Juvencus Manuscript in the University of Cambridge Library there are two collections of *englynion* (strict metre quatrains), one from the 9th century and the other from the 10th. Also, in the same university there is a fragment of a treatise on astronomy dating from the 10th century. An interesting feature of the language at the beginning this period was that words were accentuated on the last syllable. By the end of the Old Welsh period, however, the emphasis had shifted to the penultimate syllable, where it remains, by and large, to this day.

A great deal of poetry from this period was retained orally and written down in later periods. Some of the literary treasures of the language, such as the Book of Aneirin, the Book of Taliesin and the poems relating to Llywarch Hen and Heledd, are notable examples.

MIDDLE WELSH

There is plenty of evidence, by this period, to suggest that Welsh had developed into a rich and flexible language, capable of being used in a variety of ways. If the work of the Poets of the Princes (*Gogynfeirdd*) was written in an antiquated, conservative idiom, the laws of Hywel Dda bear testimony to the fact that Welsh had an extensive vocabulary, capable of conveying the most complex legal concepts, while the tales of the Mabinogi showed that it was also an effective medium for relating stories and entertaining an audience.

One interesting feature of the language in this period was the use of the third person past-tense ending *–wys*. It is worth noting that this ending is still preserved in the spoken dialect of West Glamorgan, where people will often say '*Fe godws e*' (*He rose*) rather than the more usual, '*Fe gododd e*'.

MODERN WELSH

The work of Dafydd ap Gwilym, Wales' greatest poet, is an important milestone in the development of the language. He used the living language in his *cywyddau*, setting a standard to which his successors aspired. It was this language, the language of the poets, which Bishop Morgan later used in his masterly translation of the Bible into Welsh in 1588. This happened at a time when Welsh had lost its status and patronage, after the passing of the Acts of Union, and when the language was in danger of disintegrating into a number of dialects. During this period, the vocabulary was enriched, especially through borrowing from English; there was more uniformity in the form of verbs and prepositions, and patterns of mutation became more standardised. Like every other living language, Welsh continues to change and develop to this day, proving that it can react to the complex demands of this age of electronic communication.

The Romans

To what extent did the Roman occupation influence the language?

In May, 43AD, the Romans, under the command of Aulus Platus, attacked Britain. Three months later, it was safe enough for the Emperor Claudius to visit these islands. He was carried into Camulodunum (Colchester) on the back of an elephant, and by about 70 AD, the whole island, apart from the north of Scotland, was under the authority of the Romans. They called this new state Britannia. Brythonic was the language spoken by the indigenous population, but as these people came into contact with Latin they borrowed many words from that language.

The first Romans who arrived were soldiers, and for many years Rome was synonymous with the military in the minds of the Welsh. As these soldiers had money, the Brythonic peoples established villages near their centres of settlement, in order to trade. They also noticed that the Romans' method of fighting, together with their arms, were very different from the British. It is little wonder, therefore, that words like *castell* (castle), *mur* (wall), *pebyll* (tents) *ffos* (ditch) *llurig* (chain-mail) and *saeth* (arrow), which later became an integral part of the Welsh language, were borrowed from the Romans.

The lifestyle of the Romans was very different from that of the British, who were anxious to emulate their conquerors. Because of this, words like *cegin* (kitchen), *ffwrn* (oven), *ystafell* (room), *ffenest* (window), *torch* (torque) and *maneg* (glove) became a part of their vocabulary. They began to drink *gwin* (wine) and eat *torth* (a loaf) and *selsig* (sausage).

17

They borrowed words relating to work and trade, such as *aur* (gold), *plwm* (lead), *pwys* (a pound weight) and *mesur* (measure), as well as many words relating to religious matters: *angel* (angel), *clas* (close, or cloister), *diafol* (devil), *efengyl* (gospel) and *eglwys* (church).

It became fashionable to give children Latin names, and in time Welsh children were called Meirion, Garmon, Dinawd and Tegid. In the field of education, the words *disgybl* (pupil), *gramadeg* (grammar), *llên* (literature), *llyfr* (book), *gwers* (lesson), *ysgol* (school) and *ysgrifennu* (to write), were borrowed.

It is probable that many of the indigenous British population were bilingual, especially those living near towns and those who were anxious to succeed in the new world that was developing around them.

When the Romans left Britain in 410, the influence of Latin declined. Although it was used in the church, the monasteries and schools, it wasn't a living community language. Brythonic was the everyday language of the people and it was spoken across the major part of the island. At this time, it was possible to travel from Edinburgh to Cornwall, and speak some form of Brythonic all along the way.

When the Romans left these shores, it must have seemed that the problems facing the native Brythons would disappear, but that was far from true, as we shall see.

The Arrival
of the Anglo-Saxons

What became of the Celtic languages with the arrival of the Anglo-Saxons?

It is possible that you have been to Nant Gwrtheyrn on the Llŷn Peninsula. If not, it would be worth your while visiting this interesting, remote village, which has been developed as a language centre that offers Welsh language courses throughout the year. Near the village there is a huge rock with a sheer drop to the sea below. The rock is known as *Y Garreg Llam* (The Leaping Stone). According to tradition, it was from this rock that Vortigern (Gwrtheyrn) leapt to his death. But who was Vortigern?

After the Romans left Britain, the Picts to the north and the Irish to the west were a threat to the native British population. Tradition has it that Vortigern (Gwrtheyrn) was one of the leaders of the country who foolishly decided to ask two Anglo-Saxon chieftains, Hengist and Horsa, for help to defend his territory against these enemies. In exchange for their assistance, he offered them money and land. Together, they succeeded in defeating the Picts and the Irish, but the Saxons grew so fond of the country that they decided to stay, taking land from the native population and establishing a kingdom in south-east England. In his anguish, Vortigern fled to Llŷn and ended his life by leaping from *Y Garreg Llam*.

That's the legend, but, as a matter of fact, it is probable that soldiers from those parts of Europe we refer to as Germany and The Netherlands had come to Britain with the Roman armies.

Even while the Romans were here, they had to build forts along the eastern seaboard in order to repel the attacks of these people. When the Romans left these islands in 410 AD, the Saxons began to cross the sea once more, establishing settlements in eastern England. Gradually, they branched out across the country, assimilating the natives as they went. They had reached the Severn estuary by 577 and the estuary of the Dee by 616, thus separating the native people into three disparate groups – one in the north of England, one in Wales and the third in Cornwall.

In time, the languages of these groups developed in their own ways, giving us Welsh in Wales and Cornish in the south-west. Wealas (later, Welsh) was the name by which the Saxons referred to Wales. The meaning of that word was foreigner. The same element is to be found in the English words walnut (a foreign nut), and Walloons (foreign people) in Belgium. In the eyes of the Saxons, therefore, we were foreigners in our own country. On the other hand, the Welsh called themselves, *Cymry*, which means compatriots, or people related to one another.

Of the three Brythonic languages on mainland Britain, only Welsh is spoken today. Although farmers in the north-west of England have a system of counting sheep similar to that of Welsh, and although place names such as Elmet, Penrith and Ecclefechan testify that a language related to Welsh was once spoken in northern England and southern Scotland, it is probable that that language died out in the 11th century. Welsh, therefore, is the oldest language on the British mainland, much older than English and Scottish Gaelic, which are both just 1500 years old.

The Celts and the English

The Language in Action

What was the state of Welsh before 1536?

During the Middle Ages and for some considerable time afterwards, Welsh was not only spoken in Wales itself but also to the east of Offa's Dyke, in parts of the present-day English counties of Hereford and Shropshire.

Although Welsh had a number of lively and colourful dialects, the written language was quite standardised when compared with other languages, such as English. Welsh was the only language spoken by most of the population and was, therefore, used to discuss every aspect of life. From this period we have many translations, as well as original works dealing with a wide variety of subjects.

Brut y Tywysogion (The Chronicle of the Princes) is a good example of a history book written in Welsh, and the laws of Hywel Dda demonstrate that Welsh, even at that early time, was a flexible language that had developed a rich vocabulary that was capable of dealing with the most complex subjects. These included hunting, heraldry, husbandry, medicine and geography. Welsh was also used regularly in drawing up title deeds.

Naturally, this period produced a great deal of creative writing in prose and verse. One of Wales' greatest contributions to European literature is *The Mabinogion*, a collection of thirteen tales full of wonderful characters and exciting incident. These stories were very old and, originally, they would have been related orally by story-tellers who entertained generations of people, in the courts of the princes, or on the hearth of ordinary homes. Sometime between 1050 and 1170, a talented, anonymous writer (or writers) recorded

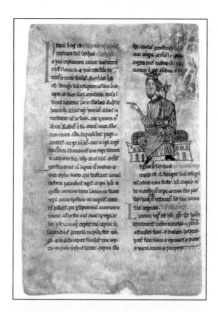

Illustrations from the law books of Hywel Dda

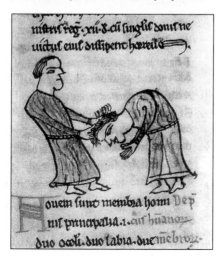

and edited the tales, and they continue to fascinate people even to this day.

Every year, at the National Eisteddfod, the winning poet is still chaired in a ceremony that reminds us of the poet's traditionally high standing in Wales. Indeed, the *pencerdd*, or chief poet, had a special chair in the prince's court. At that time, the poet was a professional craftsman whose duties were carefully defined in the native laws.

He would have learned his craft from other poets, and, having progressed from being a pupil to the status of *bardd teulu* (family poet), he would eventually, were he good enough, attain the position of *pencerdd* or chief poet. Initially, the poets were supported by the princes but, after 1282, they had to depend on the patronage of the gentry. Recognised poets were able to go on an itinerary of the great houses, performing their poems and receiving payment for their services. It was in this period that *cynghanedd*, a system of consonance or alliteration, one of the defining features of Welsh verse, developed, together with many of the metres that are still used by poets. Although there were many excellent poets writing at this time, the ablest of them, without doubt, was Dafydd ap Gwilym. He was famous for his nature and love poetry and his willingness to write about his romantic escapades!

In Wales during the Middle Ages, most people were monoglot Welsh speakers and the language extended to every facet of their lives – their work, their religion, their health, their entertainment and all their interests. Like every other language that is afforded the opportunity, Welsh developed all the necessary resources required to fulfil this task, including a wide variety of technical terms.

The Acts of Union (1536–43)

Was the elimination of the Welsh language one of the aims of the Acts of Union?

Thomas Cromwell, Henry VIII's chief administrator, wished to create a strong, uniform and modern state in these islands by incorporating the various countries into one united kingdom. He could see this happening at this time in other countries, such as France and Spain, and had come to believe that strength lay in unity. By 1541, the Irish Parliament had accepted Henry VIII's right to call himself King of Ireland, and Cromwell knew that many Welshmen wanted to see an end to the unjust laws that they had suffered for centuries. Welshmen wished to enjoy the same privileges as the common Englishman.

The intention of the 1536 Act was to make Wales a part of England —'incorporate, unite and join' are the words used. From now on, the law of the land would be English law; new counties were created, and it became possible to bequeath property to the eldest son, rather than dividing it between all the sons, as was the traditional practice in Wales.

It was natural for English to be the official language of the country. The 1536 Act speaks of Welsh in these terms:

'the people of the same dominion have and do daily use a speche nothing like ne consonaunt to the naturall mother tonge used within this Realme'.

This wasn't to Cromwell's liking and he announced the intention of Parliament,

'utterly to extirpe alle and singular the sinister usages and customs'.

The language lost any status it formerly possessed and it became impossible for anyone who was unable to speak English to hold public office. Justices and Members of Parliament were chosen from among the English-speaking aristocracy, and those who wished their children to succeed in the new English-speaking world began sending them to be educated in England. Gradually, this class of people turned their backs on Welsh, and by the end of the 18th century very few of the gentry were able to speak the language.

Neither Henry VIII nor Thomas Cromwell deliberately sought to eliminate Welsh. Their only aim was to unify all parts of the realm and ensure that every region was administered and governed in the same way. It was important to do this through one language, and that language was to be English. That was also the policy in Ireland

An excerpt from the Act of Union 1536, referring to the language

and Calais, so it could be argued that Wales was not treated any differently. But if the Acts didn't set out intentionally to harm the language, Welsh lost status in its own country and some, especially from the higher echelons of society, began to despise it. It was at this time that Dic Sion Dafydd came to prominence – that despicable character, who wanted to forget his Welsh and turn against it as soon as he was within sight of the River Severn or the steeples of Shrewsbury.

Some of the intelligentsia could clearly foresee the danger to the language, but others welcomed the peace and the economic advantages of being on an equal footing with the English. Indeed, nobody felt disadvantaged as a result of the Acts. But as the upper class lost the language, so the poets lost their patrons and the bardic order that had maintained the standard of the language and its culture was seriously undermined. It appeared that Welsh was about to degenerate into a number of regional dialects rather than develop into a national language. But that wasn't to be.

The Translation of the Bible

Why was translation of the Bible into Welsh so important for the language?

In 1588, the Spanish Armada attacked England, but the navy, under the command of Sir Francis Drake, managed to defeat the Spaniards and save the country. In that same year there was an event of equal importance to Welsh history, for it was then that Dr William Morgan completed the translation of the Bible into Welsh, so ensuring that the language had a future.

Born in 1545, William Morgan was the son of a tenant on the Gwydir Estate in the Conway Valley. It is likely that he received his early education in the Gwydir household, before moving on to Cambridge University in 1565. There, he studied Latin, Greek and Hebrew, the original languages of the Bible, and, after graduating in 1571, he went on to be awarded his Doctorate in Divinity in 1583.

After spending four years as a deacon and priest at Ely Cathedral, near Cambridge, he returned to Wales in 1572, when he became vicar of Llanbadarn Fawr, Aberystwyth. In 1578, he was appointed vicar of Llanrhaeadr ym Mochnant, and it was there that he started on his great task of translating the Bible.

In 1563, Parliament had passed a law ordering the bishops of Wales and Hereford to ensure that Welsh translations of the Bible and the Book of Common Prayer were available by 1567, so that services in the Welsh-speaking areas could be conducted in the vernacular. This arose, not out of love of the Welsh language, but at a time when there was religious dissonance throughout Europe.

It is likely that Parliament had concluded that ensuring religious stability was more important than attaining linguistic uniformity. It was also hoped that placing a Welsh version of the Bible beside its English equivalent in every church would help monoglot Welsh speakers to learn English.

The title page of William Morgan's Bible

The memorial in St. Asaph to the translators of the Bible.

William Salesbury had been mainly responsible for the translation of the New Testament and the Prayer Book that had been published in 1567. Although the translation was of a high standard, many people disliked its Latinate orthography, Salesbury's use of obsolete words and his refusal to notate certain mutations.

However, in 1588, William Morgan's *tour de force* made its appearance. He used the classical language of the poets, and although this must have sounded strange to most people at the outset, they soon became accustomed to its majestic rhythms as they listened to it every Sunday in churches throughout Wales. As well as being a scholar, William Morgan was a talented writer. His feat in translating the whole Bible was incredible, considering that he completed much of the work in the remote parish of Llanrhaeadr ym Mochnant, far from any library. In addition, during his period at Llanrhaeadr, he faced many serious personal problems at the very time that he was trying to complete his *magnum opus*.

William Morgan's translation had a profound influence on the future of the Welsh language. Common folk in all parts of the country heard the pure literary language that he borrowed from the poets and, as a result, Welsh did not disintegrate into a multitude of dialects, as happened with Irish and Scottish Gaelic. This is an important factor when we consider how Welsh succeeded in keeping its identity.

Following his translation of the Bible, William Morgan was appointed Bishop of Llandaff in 1595 and Bishop of St. Asaph in 1601. He died, a comparatively poor man, in 1604, leaving an estate worth £110. If you visit St. Asaph, remember to visit the cathedral. In front of that church there stands a memorial to the translators of the Bible with William Morgan a giant in their midst – one of the greatest benefactors of the Welsh language.

The Educational Movements, 1660–1760

Why were so many people able to read Welsh by the end of the 18th century?

Between the middle of the seventeenth and the middle of the eighteenth centuries three important educational movements were established in Wales. All three were voluntary movements and two were primarily established by Englishmen who were concerned by the pitiful moral state of the Welsh people

The first of these movements was the Welsh Trust, established in 1674. Its main promoter was a London clergyman, Thomas Gouge. The Trust opened schools for poor children in order to teach them to read, write and count. Its aim was to teach the tenets of the Protestant faith and to protect the populace from Catholicism. Schools were opened throughout the length and breadth of Wales and, by 1675, 2,225 children were receiving a free education. At the outset, both Anglicans and Nonconformists co-operated happily, but, in time, some became suspicious of Thomas Gouge's motives, claiming that he was too biased in favour of Nonconformists. The Welsh language was another problem. To people like Gouge, the language was a nuisance, but parents, on the other hand, were unwilling for their children to be taught in English, a language that the vast majority didn't understand.

Some of the Welsh people who worked for the Trust thought likewise. One of these was Stephen Hughes, a Carmarthen

Nonconformist. He recognised that it was essential to use Welsh as a means of saving souls, and saw the need to publish religious books in the language in order to do this effectively. Hughes published a number of books, including the Book of Psalms, the New Testament and an edition of 8,000 Bibles, in 1678. This helped to ensure a certain amount of Welsh in the voluntary schools. However, the Welsh Trust was wound up in 1681 when Gouge died.

In 1699, the Society for the Promotion of Christian

Welch Piety was Griffith Jones's annual report to his sponsors

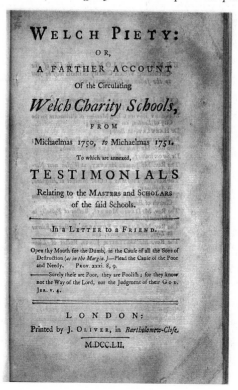

Knowledge, or SPCK, was established by four English people and one Welshman. The industrialist, Sir Humphrey Mackworth, was the sole Welshman involved but, later, Sir John Phillips of Picton Castle in Pembrokeshire played a leading role in the work of the Society in Wales. As with the Welsh Trust, reading, writing and arithmetic formed the basis of the curriculum, although boys were also taught a craft and the girls instructed in knitting and sewing. The teacher was usually the parish priest, and classes were held in the churches. Between 1699 and 1740, 96 schools were established in Wales.

These schools were less successful after 1715, when many Nonconformists refused to support them. Once more, the matter of using English as the medium of instruction became a burning issue, and poor parents were reluctant to allow their children to attend school when their help was required at home.

From 1708, the teacher in the SPCK school in Laugharne was one of the great Welshmen of the eighteenth century, Griffith Jones, Llanddowror. He was a powerful and popular preacher and because he was married to Margaret, sister of Sir John Phillips of Picton Castle, he received a great deal of help from that influential gentleman. Griffith Jones soon saw that it was pointless to try to teach monoglot Welsh children through the medium of English. In 1731, therefore, he opened his own school in Llanddowror with the intention of teaching people of all ages how to read. That was the beginning of the circulating schools in Wales. They were wholly pragmatic, as teaching people to read was their only aim, with courses usually lasting just three months. As country people were busy during the summer, classes were usually held during the winter and sometimes of an evening, when the day's work was over.

By 1737, Griffith Jones had established 27 schools, with 2,400 pupils in attendance. Many of these were adults. Teachers were paid £3 - £4 per annum, and Griffith Jones established a training academy for them at Llanddowror, in order to ensure that they were effectively prepared. Because of the esteem in which he was held, Jones attracted many talented teachers, despite the paltry remuneration, and he also persuaded a number of wealthy English people to support the schools. In addition to Sir John Phillips, Madam Bridget Bevan also offered him valuable assistance. He depended on her greatly as he didn't enjoy good health and many people added to his problems by accusing him of using the schools to further the cause of Methodism.

When Griffith Jones died in 1761, it was said that he had established about 3,325 schools since 1737, attended by 200,000 children and adults. Unlike the Welsh Trust and SPCK, these schools gave the Welsh language its rightful recognition, and Griffith Jones succeeded in creating a literate population. News of his achievement travelled far and in 1764 Catherine of Russia sent emissaries to Wales to report on these successful schools.

The Treachery
of the Blue Books

What was the Treachery of the Blue Books?

Following a speech in the House of Commons in 1846 by William Williams, a Welshman from Llanpumsaint, Carmarthenshire, a commission was established to inquire into the state of education in Wales and particularly the opportunities afforded to ordinary workers to learn English. The government was concerned with law and order in Wales at this time, in the wake of the Chartist uprising in the south-east and the Rebecca Riots in the west of the country. It was little wonder, therefore, that they were prepared to listen to the concerns of Williams, who was the MP for Coventry.

By 1 April 1847, the commissioners had compiled a report of 1,252 pages, published in three volumes. Its content aroused a storm of protest in Wales and in time the whole episode was referred to as the 'Treachery of the Blue Books'.

The authors of the report were three young English barristers, Lingen, Symons and Johnson. They spoke no Welsh and were unable to understand the language although, at this time, the majority of working class people in Wales were monoglot Welsh speakers. Also, the commissioners were churchmen, whereas the majority of ordinary Welsh people were Nonconformists.

The report painted a sorry picture of the state of education in Wales. It stated that a high percentage of adults were unable to write their names and many children didn't attend school at all. Often, private schools were housed in inadequate premises and, on the whole, the standard of education was very low. The only schools available in all parts of the country were the Sunday Schools that, incidentally, were praised by the commissioners for teaching both children and adults to read Welsh and affording them the opportunity to discuss all manner of subjects. However, in their view, even this education was very restricted. In taking evidence, the commissioners had to rely on interpreters who were often incompetent. Sometimes, they questioned children about things they hadn't learned, and they were extremely critical of the teachers' ability to teach English as a second language. At the same time, they saw nothing wrong with children being taught through the medium of a language they were unable to understand. The commissioners paid too much attention to the evidence of Anglicans, who were a minority in Wales and were always ready to find fault with those who attended chapels. The report claimed that Welsh people were dirty, lazy, drunk, ignorant and immoral, and attributed this to two factors, namely, the Welsh language and the chapel. Indeed, they even claimed that chapel meetings were merely an excuse for young people to meet one another in order to participate in immoral acts.

This is the part of the report that attracted most attention in the London press and also the part that most annoyed the Welsh populace. People were incensed that Welsh women, in particular, had been maligned and many leapt to their defence. One of the most effective voices raised against the report was that of Ieuan Gwynedd (Evan Jones 1820 – 52), a young journalist, who showed that many of the facts it contained were inaccurate.

There is no doubt that the Blue Books affair had a great effect on the attitude of Welsh people. Most of the leaders of the country were sensitive to the criticism it contained and they attempted to demonstrate that the Welsh were honest, moral and respectable people. On the other hand, the event caused some like the radical patriot, Rev. Michael D. Jones to become more nationalistic in outlook. As compulsory education became established in the last quarter of the century, Welsh people, by and large, were happy for schools to promote English at the expense of Welsh. From then on, the aim of education was to prepare children to take their place in an English-speaking world. In the field of religion, however, the gulf between church and chapel widened, with chapels becoming bastions of the language. This was largely the position until the middle of the twentieth century.

One of Hugh Hughes's cartoons depicting the Treachery of the Blue Books

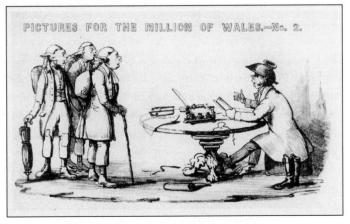

Welsh in the Twentieth Century

What happened to the language during the 20th century, and what are its prospects now?

Since the beginning of the last century, the number and percentage of Welsh speakers decreased in each consecutive Census up to 1991. Here are the figures for each decade:

1901 – 929,824 (49.9%)
1911 – 977,366 (43.5%)
1921 – 922,092 (37.1%)
1931 – 909,261 (36.8%)
1951 – 714,686 (28.9%)
1961 – 656,002 (26%)
1971 – 542,425 (20.9%)
1981 – 503,520 (19%)
1991 – 508,098 (18.6%)
2001 – 582,368 (20.8%)

You will notice that between 1981-91 the percentile decrease was less than in previous Censuses and, for the first time since Census returns have been recorded in Wales, the 2001 statistics showed that both the number and percentage of Welsh speakers had actually increased. The traditional heartlands of the north and west remain the strongest areas. Although the percentage of Welsh speakers only exceeds 65% in one area, namely Gwynedd, there are large clusters of speakers in Carmarthenshire (83,802), Ceredigion (37,772), Ynys

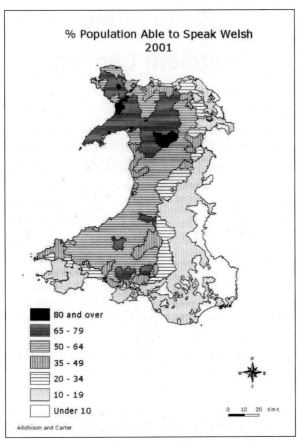

The Welsh Language in 2001
(from Spreading the Word, *Aitchison and Carter, Y Lolfa)*

Môn (38,709) and Conwy (31,042). It should also be noted that both Cardiff (31,944) and Swansea (28,581), Wales's largest cities, have substantial Welsh-speaking populations. Although Welsh has been traditionally associated with rural areas, most speakers of the language now dwell in urban settlements. However, those communities where Welsh is the natural, every-day means of communication are generally located in rural Wales.

The name given to this area is *Y Fro Gymraeg* (The Welsh-speaking Area). Although the percentage of speakers living in *Y Fro* has fallen with each consecutive Census, it is possible to define the *Bro Gymraeg* as an area covering a large part of the landmass of Wales. After the 1951 Census, however, it became apparent that this amorphous geographical area was beginning to break up into a series of separate 'lakes' or 'islands', and it is by now difficult to think of it as an uniform linguistic area. In 1961, Welsh speakers were in the majority over 57% of the land surface of Wales. By 1971 this had fallen to 47%, but there were still 279 communities where 80% of the people spoke Welsh. By 1981 there were only 66 such communities and this number fell to 32 by 1991. This number had decreased further, to 17 wards by 2001, all of which were located within Gwynedd and Ynys Môn. The good news emanating from the 1991 Census, however, was that there was an increase in the number of young Welsh-speakers. In that year, 22% of Welsh speakers were under 15 years of age, compared with 21.7% over 65. Between 1981 and 1991, the number of young speakers increased by 22.8%. In Gwent, Mid-Glamorgan and South Glamorgan, 30% of Welsh speakers were under 15 years of age. This trend continued during the following decade, and it is interesting to note that, in 2001, 41.6% of Welsh-speakers in Cardiff were aged between 16 and 44.

Although inward migration has weakened the language in some areas, it is interesting to note that in 1991 almost 10% of Welsh speakers (48,919) were born outside Wales. This suggests that many of those who choose to come to live here make an effort to learn the language. This also shows how methods of teaching the language have improved.

As Cardiff has developed as a capital city and became an administrative, educational and cultural centre, the number of Welsh speakers has increased from 9,623 in 1951 to 18,071 by 1991. As we have seen, that number rose to 31,944 by 2001, an increase of nearly 77%, or 10.9% of the population of the capital. Many people have come from other parts of Wales to work in the media, education and administration. They are mainly educated, middle-class people in safe jobs, who are prepared to demand their rights. It is no accident that it is in Cardiff that the first Welsh language community newspaper was established and it is there also that the idea of establishing a Welsh playgroup movement (*Mudiad Ysgolion Meithrin*) was initiated.

It is likely that the importance of Welsh in Cardiff will increase as the National Assembly grows in influence and as the city develops into a true capital of the country.

The rural areas have their problems. Because of the lack of work, young people move away, to be replaced by incomers attracted by comparatively cheap housing and the beautiful countryside. As some of these fail to realise that they live in a country with its own language and culture, there has been friction from time to time in the past, especially in the field of education.

Although the future of the language is uncertain, experts are of the opinion that the 2001 Census marks an upturn in its fortunes. Despite a decline in the number of speakers in the traditionally Welsh-speaking areas, the gains in the rest of Wales appear to have more than made up for these losses.

Saunders Lewis and the 'Fate of the Language'

Why was Saunders Lewis's radio lecture, 'The Fate of the Language' such an important event for the Welsh language?

In the middle of the fifties, the city of Liverpool announced that it required more water for industry. After considering a number of possible ways to meet this demand, they decided that the best option was to drown the Tryweryn valley, near the town of Bala in Merionethshire. The only village in the valley was Capel Celyn, a completely Welsh-speaking community that comprised a few houses, a post office, a chapel and a school. There was a huge protest when Liverpool's intentions became apparent, with all Welsh Members of Parliament, with one exception, voting against the scheme when it came before the House. Despite the protests, and efforts to obstruct the project illegally, including the deployment of sabotage, by 1963 the valley had been drowned.

Many were concerned with the state of the Welsh language at the time, and Tryweryn became a symbol of the dangers Welsh-speaking areas were facing. To many, democratic means of defending Wales had failed, and it appeared that the efforts of Plaid Cymru, the political party that had protested loudest against the scheme, had been futile.

It was early in 1962, when the morale of the country was at a low ebb, and the results of the Census were about to be announced, that Saunders Lewis was invited to deliver the BBC's annual St

David's Day Lecture.

In the eyes of many, Saunders Lewis was the greatest Welshman of his generation. The son of a Nonconformist minister, he had been born and educated on Merseyside. After serving as an officer in the First World War, he graduated in English at the University of Liverpool and was then appointed lecturer in Welsh at the University College of Wales, Swansea. In 1925, he was one of the group of patriots who established *Plaid Genedlaethol Cymru* (The

Saunders Lewis

National Party of Wales) that later became Plaid Cymru. In 1936, he was imprisoned for his part in the arson attack on the 'Bombing School' on the Llŷn Peninsula, an act that cost him his lectureship at Swansea. From then until 1952, he earned a precarious living by writing, farming and teaching, but in that year he was appointed to the Department of Welsh at University College, Cardiff where he remained until his retirement in 1957.

As well as being a prominent politician, Saunders Lewis had established a reputation as a playwright, novelist, poet, journalist and literary critic. He was highly respected, even by those who didn't subscribe to his political ideas. For that reason, when he was invited to deliver the annual St David's Day lecture, and chose as his subject, 'The Fate of the Language', people were anxious to hear his message. The main thrust of his argument on 13 February 1962, was that it should be made impossible for central and local government to function without Welsh. As an example of this, he spoke of the heroic struggle of Trefor and Eileen Beasley, Llangennech, in their efforts to compel the Llanelli Rural District Council to issue rate papers in Welsh. He claimed that, in order to implement such a radical policy, a revolution would be necessary, the catalyst of which would be a movement that would be prepared to use revolutionary methods. The movement he had in mind was Plaid Cymru, but in the opinion of the president of that party, Gwynfor Evans, it was not possible for a political party to concentrate on a single issue, namely the Welsh language. However, as a result of the lecture, a number of young people got together during the summer of 1962 and established one of the most important language movements of the twentieth century, *Cymdeithas yr Iaith Gymraeg* – The Welsh Language Society.

Cymdeithas yr Iaith /
The Welsh Language Society

How was Cymdeithas yr Iaith Gymraeg established and what has it achieved so far?

When Plaid Cymru made it clear that it was unable to concentrate solely on the language issue, a number of young nationalists decided to establish *Cymdeithas yr Iaith Gymraeg* (The Welsh Language Society). That happened in the summer of 1962.

Most of the members were university students and the object of their first campaign was to compel courts to issue summonses in Welsh. In February 1963, there were further protests in Aberystwyth, where campaigners organised a sit-in on the main

A Cymdeithas yr Iaith demonstration for a Welsh Language Act in central London, 1993

road into the town from the south, near Trefechan Bridge, thereby disrupting the traffic. This protest received a great deal of publicity in the media, but having succeeded in their campaign for Welsh summonses, the protesters turned their attention to other matters, such as the disregard of Welsh by the Post Office and the absence of the language on car licences and directional road signs. The sixties was a period of student protest throughout Europe, but it was the language that was given most prominence in Wales.

There were numerous court cases against members of the Society, and many were imprisoned. Although the majority of those involved in these campaigns were young, they were supported by a number of intellectuals, such as Saunders Lewis himself, the philosopher, J R Jones, and the astute journalist, Alwyn D Rees. On one occasion, justices of the peace contributed towards the payment of the fine imposed upon one of the leaders of the Society, triggering his release from prison.

By the seventies, the main objective of the Society was to ensure the establishment of a Welsh-language television channel.

Once more the property of the BBC and the independent channels was attacked, and, as happened previously, the

The protest on Trefechan Bridge, Aberystwyth, in 1963

Society won the support of many older people who were prominent in national life. Cymdeithas yr Iaith realised that there were many factors undermining the Welsh language, and it began campaigning in other fields, such as education, planning, the economy and establishing housing societies. There was a strong campaign against holiday homes, with many of them being occupied by protesters. The Society also supported the parents at Bryncroes on the Llŷn Peninsula, when the Education Authority threatened to close the local school.

Another campaign that attracted a great deal of publicity and aroused widespread public disapproval was the protest against the Investiture of the Prince of Wales in Caernarfon Castle in 1969. Although some factions had tried to use violence to prevent the Investiture, the Welsh Language Society used non-violent means of protest. These were the methods that had been used by the Society since its inception and which had won it a great deal of respect from the public at large.

Cymdeithas yr Iaith was basically a youth movement that initiated a number of interesting developments, such as a pop record industry, Welsh-medium education and Welsh bookshops. By today the Welsh language is a lot more visible, on road signs, in shops, in the press, in advertisements and on television. Some county councils operate a wholly bilingual policy, and the government has established the Welsh Language Board to advise the Secretary of State and the Assembly Government on matters relating to the language. Simultaneous translation enables Welsh to be used by members of the Assembly on all occasions. It would be difficult to see how all this could have happened without the determined lobbying of Cymdeithas yr Iaith and the selfless sacrifices of its young members.

Personal Names

What is the significance of ap/ab in some personal names?

Of late, more people have reverted to the traditional method of naming children. The custom in past times was for the child to take on the father's name. For example, if the father, Owain, named his son Hywel, the boy would be known as Hywel ab Owain. The *'ab'* corresponds to 'mac' in Scotland and Ireland and simply means 'son of'. The original form would have been, Hywel *fab* Owain, but as the f tends to disappear in spoken Welsh, it became *ab*.

At first, *vch*, an abbreviation of *verch*, was used when referring to females, but in time ab/ap came to be used for both sexes. This method of nomenclature was in general use up until the passing of the Acts of Union, but, after that event, the English method of using a surname became more common. That is how the Christian name David, or Dafydd, became Davies, John > Jones and Huw > Hughes. This change occurred in the 16th century, in the case of Welsh people who moved to England. Indeed, some claim that it was William ap John Thomas, a standard bearer in the court of Henry VIII, who first did this, when he changed his name to William Jones. Whether or not that is true, the trend became fashionable in Wales during the 17th century and, by the 18th, there were very few people using the traditional method.

It was customary to use 'ab' before a vowel – Dafydd ab Edmwnd – and 'ap' before a consonant – Dafydd ap Gwilym. Often, in adopting the English method, 'ab/ap' would be incorporated in the new name, so that ab Owen and ap Rhisiart became Bowen and

Pritchard, whilst the anglicised forms of ap Rhys and ab Ifan were Price and Bevan. In all probability, the English surnames Upjohn and Uprichard are also examples of keeping 'ap' at the beginning of a name.

In the process of creating new names, Welsh people would sometimes use other methods. One favoured strategy was to take the name of the family home or even the name of a town, village, area or estate, to create names such as Mostyn or Pennant. That is why such names as Powys (Powis), Gower and Lougher are now quite common.

Sometimes an adjective, descriptive of the person, would be used. From *'gwyn'* (fair / white) came the surnames Gwyn, Gwynn, Gwynne, Wyn, Wynn and Wynne, whilst *'llwyd'* (grey) gave us Lloyd and Floyd. Gooch, Gough and Goff come from *'coch'* (red), while Vaughan derives from 'fychan' (small), Dee from *'du'* (black), Voyle from *'moel'* (bald), and in various parts of Wales *Annwyl / Anwyl* (dear / affectionate), *Landeg* (handsome) and *Tew / Dew* (fat) are to be found.

Sometimes a family would adopt the name of the father's craft. The surname *Saer* (carpenter / joiner) is a good example of this; and another interesting group of names are those based on pet names. In contemporary Wales, we are familiar with Ifan becoming Ianto and Griffith becoming Guto, but when Iorwerth and Meredudd were popular boys' names, they would be changed to Iolo and Bedo respectively. As a result, we now have the surnames Beddoe, Beddow and Beddoes from Bedo and Gittins or Gittings from Guto.

Many modern Welsh surnames end in 's' – Richards, Edwards, Evans, Roberts. This is the possessive use of 's' that one sees in 'Tom's family', and this is the function it had originally, when new surnames were formed. The meaning of Evans is 'Evan's family' and Davies 'the family of David or Dafydd'.

You will see from this that our names have an important historical significance, and in using 'ap' today, people are just reverting to the method of nomenclature used by their forefathers.

Dialects of Welsh

Does the language have many dialects?

Dialect is the spoken form of a language that is peculiar to a particular area or region, or is spoken by a specific social class. Every dialect has its own vocabulary, grammar and sound system. Because of this, listening to the way people speak gives us clues regarding their origins. However, because of the influence of radio and television and the fact that people are now much more mobile, the difference between dialects is becoming less significant. At the same time, new dialects are emerging; for example, amongst young people being educated in Welsh-medium schools.

Welsh has a number of dialects but the main dividing line is between the north and south of the country. Here are some examples of variations in regional vocabulary.

South	North
tad-cu (grandfather)	taid
nawr (now)	rŵan
lan (up)	i fyny
cadno (a fox)	llwynog

The 'u' sound is pronounced differently in both regions and sometimes there are also grammatical distinctions. For example, *gyda* or *'da* are used in the south to indicate possession, whilst people in the north use various forms of *gan*. In the north, *ddaru* + *i* are used to form the past tense of verbs – *Ddaru iddo fo fynd ddoe* (He went yesterday).

However, it would be too simplistic to say that Wales only has two dialects – north and south – because differences exist between other regions. The diphthong 'oe' becomes 'we' in south Ceredigion and Pembrokeshire, with, *'Oes, oes'* (Yes, yes) becoming 'Wes, wes'; 'oer' (cold) being pronounced 'wer'; and 'oen' (lamb) > wen. In the south-east and in parts of mid-Wales, the long vowel sound, 'a' becomes 'e' – tân (fire) > tên; cân (a song) > cên and mân (small) > mên.

Linguists refer to six main dialects based in the north, centre and south of the country, with each region split into an eastern and western area. Sometimes a particular word will enable you to locate the precise location of a speaker. Take the various words used for sweets, for example. If the speaker uses *da-da* or *pethau da,* you can be fairly sure that he comes from the north-west. A speaker using *fferins* will certainly come from the north-east; *taffish* is said in west Glamorgan or east Carmarthenshire; *cacen* comes from Montgomeryshire; *candi(s)* from south Ceredigion; and *cisys* from the valleys to the east of Aberystwyth. In Bernard Shaw's play, *Pygmalion*, Professor Henry Higgins claimed to be able to locate a person to within six miles of his home and, in London, to within two streets! For reasons previously mentioned, that task isn't quite as easy nowadays, but it is interesting to try to guess from where someone comes just by listening to the words and sentence patterns used and the way that they are pronounced.

The spoken language is the foundation of all languages, although some are wont to believe that the written word is more correct or even 'better'. We must remember, however, that many ancient forms have been preserved in our dialects. In west Glamorgan, for example, people still say *acha* (on) as in *acha beic* (on a bike); *acha dydd Iau* (on Thursday), without realising that this form comes from the Middle Welsh, *ar uchaf*. In the same way, *whilia* (to speak or converse') that is used in the same area also comes from *chwedleua* in Middle Welsh. Try to listen carefully to people speaking and you will hear some very interesting things!

Welsh-medium Schools

Do many schools in Wales teach through the medium of the Welsh language?

Although primary schools in the Welsh-speaking areas used the language as a medium of instruction before any officially designated Welsh-medium schools were established, English was the language used in all other schools.

The first official *Ysgol Gymraeg* (Welsh School) was opened in Aberystwyth in 1939. It was a private school that was opened because of circumstances that arose when evacuees were moved from England to Wales at the beginning of the Second World War. There were two main problems. Firstly, there were far too many children in the local school and, secondly, there was a great deal more English to be heard around the playground. As a result, a group of parents, led by Sir Ifan ab Owen Edwards, the founder of *Urdd Gobaith Cymru* (The Welsh League of Youth), decided to establish a wholly Welsh-medium, private school. The venture was extremely successful and, as a result, parents in other areas began to ask education authorities to open similar schools.

The first authority to respond was Carmarthenshire, who opened Ysgol Dewi Sant, Llanelli, in 1947. Other counties followed suit, particularly Flint and Glamorgan. At the outset, only children from Welsh-speaking homes were accepted and, as a result, the numbers involved were small. For example, there were only 12 children in the *Ysgol Feithrin* (Nursery School) at Maesteg in 1947 and 8 at Mold in 1949. However, because of their acknowledged educational excellence, non-Welsh-speaking parents began to lobby for their children to be admitted. When their wish was granted, the schools began to expand rapidly. By 1964 there were 256 children in Ysgol Gymraeg Maesteg, and 128 in Mold. By the middle of the seventies, there were 61 official Welsh-medium schools in Wales, attended by 8,500 children.

The influence of parents on the development of these schools has been very important. It is mainly through parental pressure that they were established in the first place, and that is why the provision of Welsh-medium education varies from area to area. Sometimes, there were angry protests against certain authorities. For example, parents staged a sit-in, for some weeks at the beginning of the eighties, at Pont Sion Norton School, Pontypridd, when the Glamorgan Education Authority decided to establish Welsh-medium units, rather than schools, in the district.

The Welsh school movement was given a considerable boost in 1971, when a group of parents decided to establish *Mudiad Ysgolion Meithrin* (MYM) (Welsh Nursery Group Movement). At the time, there were 68 independent playgroups scattered throughout Wales but, after formalising the organisation, their number grew rapidly. By September 2005, MYM was responsible for 550 groups, catering for circa 10,000 children and 450 *Ti a Fi* (Toddler Groups for children under 2.5 years), attended by 6,823 children. Naturally, as a result of this growth, there was an increase in the demand for Welsh-medium education.

The influence of Welsh-medium schools has been great. In Cardiff, for example, the first school opened in 1949, with just 18 pupils. By September 2005, there were 10 primary schools catering for 2,830 children. In addition, there were 1,877 pupils receiving their secondary education through the medium of Welsh. When the first two primary schools opened in the Rhondda Valley in 1950, there were only 49 children receiving a Welsh-medium education. By September 2005, there were 1,385 pupils attending 5 primary schools, and a further 951 in the secondary school that serves the valley. These are examples from just two areas that illustrate the influence education has had on the language. Throughout Wales in January 2004, there were 448 primary schools (28%) instructing 51,131 pupils through the medium of Welsh, together with 54 secondary schools, attended by 40,169 pupils, teaching Welsh as a first language.

Despite this success, there are many questions that remain. Will these children have an opportunity to use Welsh outside school? What sort of Welsh will they be speaking? However we answer these questions, everyone accepts that ensuring a body of young people who are able to speak Welsh is an essential prerequisite for the language to survive. Without young speakers, it has no future. The percentage of Welsh speakers aged from 3 to 15 rose in every county in Wales in the years 1981 to 1991, with 22.3% of Welsh speakers in this age-group. This rose to 31.2% by 2001. That year's Census showed that, within the main growth areas of the language, the majority of speakers are less than 16 years of age – Cardiff (39.9%), Rhondda Cynon Taf (41.9%) and Caerphilly (54.5%)

The success of these schools has also influenced education committees in the traditional Welsh-speaking areas to strengthen their policies. Welsh is the official language of most of the schools of Gwynedd. The former Dyfed Education Authority designated many of its schools as Category A, or Welsh first-language schools, and there is a similar arrangement in Powys and West Glamorgan. There is no doubt that the contribution of education to the battle of the survival of the language has been considerable.

The Eisteddfod

What takes place in an eisteddfod? For how long have eisteddfodau been held in Wales?

The eisteddfod is one of Wales' best known institutions. Eisteddfodau are held annually throughout the country, ranging from small village events to much larger festivals, such as those held in Cardigan and Anglesey. But the three eisteddfodau that receive most attention in the media are the National Eisteddfod, the Urdd National Eisteddfod and the Llangollen International Eisteddfod.

The custom of holding an eisteddfod is ancient. According to tradition, the first eisteddfod was held by Lord Rhys of Deheubarth in Cardigan, in 1176. Other important eisteddfodau were held at Carmarthen in 1451 and at Caerwys in Clwyd in 1523 and 1567. The original purpose of the eisteddfod was to organise the bardic orders, define the rules of their craft and uphold standards. As poets in the Middle Ages were paid for their work, it was important to decide who was qualified to perform in the households of the gentry who were their patrons.

By the end of the 16th century, the old bardic tradition had been weakened by the Anglicisation of the upper classes, but the poets continued to meet in hostelries, to debate, entertain and practise their craft. In the 18th century, that colourful character, Iolo Morganwg (Edward Williams), established the Gorsedd of Bards, whose ceremonies are an important part of the National Eisteddfod to this day. The bards, attired in white, blue or green robes, meet in the druidic circle, with the Archdruid presiding over the ceremony from the centrally located logan stone.

In the 1860s, *Cymdeithas yr Eisteddfod Genedlaethol* (The National Eisteddfod Society) was formed, and the first National Eisteddfod was held in Aberdare in 1861. Later, financial difficulties inhibited growth, but since the Merthyr Eisteddfod of 1881, the National Eisteddfod has been held annually, except for 1914 and 1940, when the war intervened.

Competition is an integral part of the Eisteddfod. There are competitions for soloists, choirs, elocutionists, penillion singing, dancing, writing prose, acting plays and writing poetry. But nowadays, a wide variety of fringe activities take place on the *maes* or field surrounding the main pavilion where the chief competitions and ceremonies are held. In the evenings there are plays and concerts, and there is an abundance of entertainment for young people in the form of gigs and rock sessions. The *maes* itself is spacious, accommodating a large number of stands, including those of the colleges, publishers, charities, political parties and the religious denominations, as well as national movements such as *Cymdeithas yr Iaith* and *Merched y Wawr* (the Welsh language equivalent of the W.I.)

During the week there are three important ceremonies – crowning and chairing the winning poets and honouring the best prose writer. The Archdruid presides over these ceremonies, and the members of the Gorsedd of Bards are present in their colourful attire. The National Eisteddfod is held during the first full week of August and it is an important event for Welsh people. It is held alternately in north and south Wales and is a social occasion that gives participants an opportunity to become acquainted with different parts of the country.

Since 1952, the National Eisteddfod has been an exclusively Welsh-language festival. Previously, English was used, and there were some protests when the All-Welsh Rule was established. By now, however, people see the Eisteddfod as an important institution in the fight for the survival of the language. It has become one of our national symbols, like the leek and the dragon, and it has given singers, musicians, poets and writers an opportunity to learn their craft. At the same time, it has given the Welsh public an opportunity to hear and see top-class professional artists.

Normally, over 150,000 people will visit the National Eisteddfod, with many staying in the caravan village near the eisteddfod site, or else camping nearby. Many fringe activities take place during the evening, and the local hostelries are usually full to capacity. In 2005, all the Welsh local authorities agreed to contribute £350,000 annually to the National Eisteddfod, enabling the event to be held

The hustle and bustle of the Eisteddfod field

in the less affluent parts of the country. This news was well received by all supporters of the language who look forward to one week of the year when everyone has an opportunity to live in a completely Welsh atmosphere and enjoy themselves in the sound of the language – even if it rains!

Welsh Language Publishing

How many books are published in Welsh today?

The first printed book in the Welsh language appeared in 1547 and bore the strange title, *Yn y llyfr hwn* (In this book). As a matter of fact, these were the opening words of the book, which was written by John Price of Brecon. It was a theological work whose aim was to help ordinary people to understand the Christian faith. However, it contained, in addition, advice to farmers for each month of the year as well as instruction in reading Welsh. Most of the output of the press during the 17th and 18th centuries was theological in nature and published by the various voluntary educational movements.

The 19th century was the golden age of Welsh publishing, with the Welsh radical, Thomas Gee of Denbigh the best-known figure in the field. In the period 1854-79, his company published *Y Gwyddoniadur Cymreig* (The Welsh Encyclopaedia) in 10 volumes, over 9000 pages in length. Gwasg Gee continues to publish to this day.

The years of the Second World War proved to be difficult for Welsh publishing, and by 1952 the Ready Report, commissioned by the government, warned that more Welsh language books, in greater variety, were urgently needed. The report went on to say that a Welsh Book Fund should be established, in order to support production of books for schools and the general reader. This was the first time anyone had suggested the possibility of establishing a national body to oversee publishing in the Welsh language. However, it was not until 1961 that *Cyngor Llyfrau Cymru* (The Welsh Books Council) was established, and, in the meantime,

Welsh readers had to depend on book clubs such as *Cymdeithas Llyfrau Cymry Llundain* (The London Welsh Books Society) that later developed into a more general book club.

Y Cyngor Llyfrau (The Books Council) was established with the support of the local authorities, and its primary objective was to ensure a supply of popular literature and promote its sale. In order to achieve this, the Council began to pay authors for their work and to organise competitions to attract new writers. By 1965, the Council had appointed a full-time organiser, and a Welsh Books Centre was opened in 1966, to promote the sale of books. The number of titles published was not high, as the following table shows:

1965/66	1966/67	1967/68	1968/69	1969/70
14	35	38	44	46

However, during the sixties, great efforts were made to improve the format of books, and substantial improvements were seen in this aspect of the work, despite limited resources.

The financial situation improved gradually from about 1970, as the Arts Council, central government and the county councils contributed to the venture. In 1998, the Books Council was receiving £1,300,000 to promote books. Today it is financed directly by the Welsh Assembly Government, and in 2003 received £2.8 million from that body.

From the 1960s onward, the number of Welsh bookshops increased and a number of new publishing houses were established. As it developed, the Books Council was able to offer much more help to writers, and provided increased publicity for Welsh books by organising quizzes, book festivals, competitions and discussion groups throughout Wales. Now it also organises exhibitions at international book fairs, such as London and Frankfurt. The improvement in the format of books was helped with the establishment of a Design Department, and, as the market expanded, the work of the Distribution Centre increased. In 2003-04 the Council sold 690,928 items valued at over £4,211,270 million, and 230 books and 10 magazines received grants worth £923,000. Through Book Clubs, 1020 titles were sold to 14,000 children and young people. There is no doubt that the publishing scene in Wales has been transformed since the sixties in terms of the number of books available, their standard and their design.

Radio

How much broadcasting is there in Welsh?

The first broadcasting station was opened in Cardiff on 13 February 1923, one of eight established in Britain. Of course, very few people possessed a radio set at the time and English was the normal broadcasting medium. Sometimes, a Welsh language song or item would be included, but that was all. As a matter of fact, the Cardiff station was the centre for south Wales and the west of England and, initially, there was no intention of developing an all-Wales service. Indeed, when the Swansea station opened in1924, it received most of its programmes from Daventry, the centre that produced programmes for all parts of Britain. In this early period, despite protests, the BBC provided a monolingual English language service in Wales.

The protests intensified in the thirties, with ten of the thirteen county councils calling for a better service for Wales. However, despite Scotland being given its own service, the BBC claimed that it was unable to make similar provision in Wales because of the difficult terrain.

In 1935, the BBC opened a studio in Bangor and began to broadcast more Welsh language programmes, but this didn't please listeners in the west of England. Even Sir John Reith, the Director of the BBC, who had up to that point refused to consider an autonomous arrangement for Wales, had to admit that the dual function of the station pleased nobody and, in 1937, the Welsh region of the BBC began broadcasting. An important battle had been won.

Welsh language radio reached the zenith of its popularity during the Second World War and the nineteen fifties, with writers like T. Rowland Hughes producing interesting and informative programmes. Children looked forward to such programmes as *S.O.S., Galw Gari Tryfan* and light entertainment programmes such as *Y Noson Lawen, Camgymeriadau,* that were extremely popular.

By 1953, Wales had its own Broadcasting Council and, almost at once, its members began to demand more Welsh language programmes. This was difficult, because, as in the case of television at a later date, two languages shared the same wavelength, and listeners who spoke no Welsh objected to more programmes in a language they didn't understand. A solution was found to this problem in the seventies through the utilisation of very high frequency wavebands (VHF), with English used on the medium wave and Welsh on VHF. From this arrangement, Radio Cymru and Radio Wales were established as separate entities in 1979, and Wales now has a comprehensive service in both languages.

Radio Cymru is on the air from 5 a.m. until 2 a.m. the following morning, every day of the week, offering a wide variety of programmes. The station arrived on the Freeview platform in August 2003, and in January 2004 its programmes became available on Radio Player, the on-demand service online. Radio Cymru offers a comprehensive news service, with a team of professional correspondents and a world-wide network of Welsh-speakers, whose services can be called upon as required. It has also been a boon to the Welsh record industry, particularly pop music, and it has highlighted sport. In dealing with various fields of interest, new terms had to be coined, and Radio Cymru and S4C have rendered sterling service to the language in this respect, not only by creating the new terminology but by ensuring that people become familiar with it by hearing it constantly in their homes. Welsh language programmes are also broadcast by commercial stations such as Radio Ceredigion, Red Dragon Radio (Cardiff), Radio Maldwyn and Swansea Sound.

Television

How was the Welsh language television service established?

In 1960, 60% of Welsh households had a television set. By 1969, when the percentage had risen to 92%, it was obvious that television was playing an important part in everyone's life. The BBC had been producing programmes in Welsh since 1952 when the Wenvoe transmitter opened and the independent company, TWW, did likewise when the St Hilary transmitter began operating in 1958. Between them, the BBC and commercial television were producing about twelve hours a week at the start of the sixties, but this situation was unsatisfactory. However, in 1962, BBC Wales was established.

As the English speaking majority had no wish to see Welsh programmes, there was a tendency to show them late at night, or in the afternoon, when there were few viewers. Many people adjusted their aerials to receive programmes from England, when that was practicable. This meant that they neither received Welsh news programmes nor English programmes about Wales. However, many were obliged to receive Welsh language programmes, and although these only comprised 10% of the total output, there was a great deal of protest. Whereas some wished to get rid of all Welsh language programmes, others demanded more of them at peak viewing times. It soon became obvious that the only solution was to establish a separate Welsh-language channel, and that is what eventually happened.

This arrangement failed to please everyone. When Welsh and

English programmes were interspersed, many non-Welsh speakers continued to watch. Many thought that this audience would be lost, were a separate Welsh channel to be established.

At the time, there was speculation that the BBC was about to establish a fourth channel, to cater for minority interests. It was agreed at a conference convened by the Lord Mayor of Cardiff that this should be a Welsh-medium channel in Wales, and in 1974 this was accepted by the Crawford Committee. The Labour Party accepted this decision, but, in 1974, the Conservatives won the general election that was held in May of that year.

Although the Conservative Party had supported the establishment of the Welsh channel in their election manifesto, within four months of forming a government, the Secretary of State for Wales announced that, instead of a separate channel, they would now only be strengthening the existing service. Nationalists and members of the Welsh Language Society reacted vociferously and many people decided not to renew their television licences. Others attacked television transmitters and, in May 1980, Gwynfor Evans, the President of Plaid Cymru, announced that he would go on hunger strike unless the government changed its mind.

The government feared that this would cause unrest in Wales. As well as backing from the young members of the Welsh Language Society, the campaign had won widespread support among older people, many of whom were in positions of authority. The Archbishop of Wales led a deputation of highly respected Welshmen who asked the government to reconsider its decision and, on 17 September 1980, they acceded to this request. As a result, S4C began broadcasting on 1 November 1982.

By 2003, S4C was broadcasting an average 210 hours per week in Welsh and English. Of these, an average of 21.9 hours were in Welsh, transmitted in the peak hours between 6.30 p.m. and 10.00 p.m. Since November 1998, a new digital channel has been in operation, offering 12 hours of Welsh language programmes daily. In 2003, the channel commissioned 724 hours for the digital service in addition to the simultaneous transmission of the analogue service. Since 1999, S4C has been available throughout Europe, via satellite. Despite fears that it would prove impossible for half a million people to sustain a television channel of sufficiently high standard, S4C has succeeded in creating a wide variety of excellent programmes. Its news service has received praise for bringing us reports in Welsh from all parts of the world. It has produced plays and popular drama series, including the evergreen soap opera, *Pobol y Cwm* that continues to attract a wide audience. Non-Welsh speakers have become accustomed to watching all types of sport, especially soccer and rugby, with the commentary in Welsh, and there have also been numerous programmes for Welsh learners. In this respect, the sub-titling service provided by the channel has proved to be most useful.

By now, those independent companies producing programmes for S4C have become an important part of the Welsh economy, especially in the Welsh-speaking areas, and Welsh can be counted one of the few minority European languages that can boast an independent television service.

Welsh for Adults

How much opportunity is there for adults to learn Welsh today?

Throughout the centuries, there have been examples of people moving into Wales and learning the language. This happened in the case of English people seeking work in the slate quarrying region of north Wales, and in the south Wales coalfield, during the 19th and early 20th century. That is why so many Welsh speakers have English surnames. Others learnt the language in order to read its rich literature. Among these, we can list the English writers Gerard Manley Hopkins, George Borrow and William Barnes.

Another Englishman who learnt Welsh was A S D Smith, or *Caradar*, as he was known by his bardic name. He was a teacher of modern languages at Blundell School, and it was his course, *Welsh Made Easy*, published in 1926, that was the first to seek to teach the language in a clear and orderly fashion. But even up to the middle of the last century, adults who had succeeded in learning the language were a source of wonder.

Interest in learning Welsh grew apace in the fifties and sixties, and *Cymraeg i Oedolion*, a course written by R. M. (Bobi) Jones, latterly Professor of Welsh at Aberystwyth, who had himself learnt the language, proved to be an important milestone, with its emphasis on grading the standard spoken language carefully. Another significant development was the establishment of intensive Wlpan courses. An intensive course for primary school teachers had been established at the Glamorgan Teachers' Training College, Barry, in 1966-67, and, following experiments in the Cardiff area, courses offering five 2-hour sessions a week were set up. Today there is a variety of intensive courses available throughout Wales.

In 1964 the first version of *Cymraeg Byw* was published. This was an attempt to define standard spoken Welsh. Many people criticised this synthetic language, but it was widely used by language course designers and those responsible for courses on radio and television.

In 1976, *Cyngor yr Iaith Gymraeg* (The Welsh Language Council) published its report, *Dysgu Cymraeg i Oedolion*, which called for more assistance for those learning Welsh. This report stressed the need to attract more tutors, to establish a national body responsible for the field, and for every education authority to appoint an officer responsible for Welsh for Adults.

The Welsh Joint Education Committee (WJEC) established a panel to be responsible for the field and, in time, it was able to offer a number of graded levels that led to the *Defnyddio Cymraeg* (Using Welsh) and *Defnyddio Cymraeg Uwch* (Using Welsh – Advanced) examinations. In 1984, *Cyngor y Dysgwyr* (CYD) (The Learners' Council) was formed, to promote the social use of the language. This body organises meetings where Welsh speakers and learners come together to chat informally.

The Welsh for Adults field operates under the aegis of the Welsh Language Board and its work is funded by the Welsh Further Education Funding Council. Until recently, the country was divided into eight regions, each with a consortium that coordinated the work. These consortia aimed to ensure that a variety of courses were available, that tutors received adequate training and that attainment was constantly assessed. The work was overseen by a National Officer, who initially worked through the WJEC, but who is now located in Elwa. The Officer worked in collaboration with a

The Nant Gwrtheyrn National Language Centre

National Consultative Committee and a number of sub-committees that dealt with strategy, marketing, assessment, training and research. A magazine for tutors is published regularly, and there is also an annual residential training course. Soon, these arrangements will change, with the responsibility being transferred to 6 lead bodies. The examination system will in future conform to the guidelines laid down by ALTE (The Association of Language Teachers in Europe).

A number of colleges and other bodies organise residential courses throughout the year, including a three-month residential course that is held annually at University College, Lampeter. Another exciting venture was the establishment of the Nant Gwrtheyrn Language Centre near Nefyn on the Llŷn Peninsula in

Gwynedd (Telephone: 01758 750334), where courses are available throughout the year. Welsh language courses geared for the world of work have grown in importance. There is a wide variety of books available for learners of the language, together with tapes, CDs, videos and online materials. Learners also have their own attractive magazine, called *Lingo Newydd*. With regular programmes on radio and television and back-up on the internet, there is plenty of help available, and many succeed in mastering the language in a short space of time.

Bwrdd yr Iaith Gymraeg – The Welsh Language Board

What are the main aims of the Welsh Language Board?

The Welsh Language Board was established on 21 December 1993 as a direct result of passing the Welsh Language Act in that year. The Board's main remit is to promote the use of Welsh in all aspects of daily life and to increase the numbers speaking the language.

In 1996, the Board published its *Strategy for the Welsh Language,* the aim of which was to ensure that more people spoke the language, and that they were given more opportunity to use it. To achieve success in this direction, it is necessary to change practices in language use and to ensure that it remains a living language at community level.

The 1993 Act stated that both Welsh and English should be treated equitably in Wales, and that public bodies had to prepare Language Schemes to show how they intended to achieve this. Part of the Language Board's remit is to examine these schemes and advise those providing services on matters concerning the Welsh language. After accepting a language scheme, the Board is responsible for monitoring it regularly, to ensure that it is implemented effectively. By 1998, each of the 22 county councils in Wales had prepared a scheme, as had bodies such as the Post Office, police, health trusts, the National Museum and the Countryside Council for Wales. Institutions involved in higher and further education are also required to prepare such schemes.

The Board advises the National Assembly Government on

matters relating to the language and is given money by that body to distribute to organisations involved in promoting the language, such as *Urdd Gobaith Cymru* (Welsh League of Youth), *Mudiad Ysgolion Meithrin* (Welsh Nursery Schools Movement), the National Eisteddfod, *Mentrau Iaith* (Language Ventures) and Welsh language community newspapers.

As yet, those operating in the private sector are not statutorily required to publish schemes, but the Board seeks to persuade them to do so voluntarily. Similarly, some of the utilities such as SWALEC and *Dŵr Cymru* (Welsh Water) have already published schemes. The Board has had some success in working with individual companies in the private sector, particularly in persuading stores to introduce bilingual signage.

Initially, the twelve members of the Welsh Language Board were appointed by the Secretary of State for Wales, but since 2000 this has been the responsibility of the National Assembly Government. Lord Elis Thomas was appointed as the Board's first chairman, working part-time for two days a week. The other members of the Board are required to work two days a month. Its main office is located in Cardiff and it employs 30 members of staff in its four main departments, namely Policy, Public Sector, Private Sector and Education and Training. All its activities are overseen by the Chief Executive Officer.

The Board's most practical achievements in the field are the *Mentrau Iaith* (Language Ventures) that promote the use of the language in communities such as the Gwendraeth Valley and Rhondda Cynon Taf. Here, they try to promote a variety of activities through the medium of the language, especially among young people. '*Twf*' is another innovative scheme, which seeks to persuade parents to transmit the Welsh language to the next generation. This scheme works closely with the health sector, especially midwives and field officers, to offer practical support for families wishing to pass on the Welsh language to their children.

Ultimately, the success of the Board will be measured by its ability to persuade more ordinary people to use the language. The development of language-promotion schemes will be worthless if it fails to do this. Welsh is certainly more visible than ever before – in shops, on public signage and in advertising. Its status in the field of education and public life has been enhanced, and the Welsh Language Board deserves due praise for this. Everyone wishes to see the Board succeed in its mission, but we shall have to wait some time before we can accurately measure its effectiveness at community level. In 2005 the Welsh Assembly Government decided to take the Board, together with other quangos, under its wing, a move that some see as a threat to its independence.

Children having fun on one of Menter Iaith Rhondda Cynon Taf's play schemes

The Welsh Learner's Dictionary

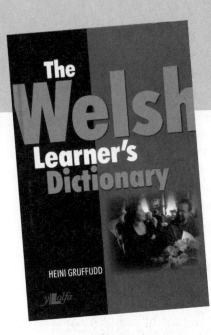

Heini
Gruffudd

The definitive dictionary for Welsh learners –
ideal for evening classes, schools, and tourists.

£3.95

ISBN: 0 86243 517 X

Welsh Rules
A Welsh Grammar for Learners

A comprehensive and genuinely useful Welsh grammar
devised especially for learners. All the elements
of this carefully graded Welsh grammar are presented
in a manner that is accessible and easy. *Welsh Rules*
is authoritative yet entertaining, and creates a new
benchmark in Welsh language learning.

£14.95

The Welsh Language is just one
of a whole range of Welsh-interest
publications from Y Lolfa. For a full list
of books currently in print, send now
for your free copy of our new, full colour
catalogue. Or simply surf into our website

www.ylolfa.com

for secure on-line ordering.

TALYBONT CEREDIGION CYMRU SY24 5AP